SUPER CITIES!

MEMPHIS

by Diane Bailey

arcadia®
CHILDREN'S BOOKS

Published by Arcadia Children's Books
A Division of Arcadia Publishing
Charleston, SC
www.arcadiapublishing.com

Super Cities is a trademark of Arcadia Publishing, Inc.

First published 2022

Manufactured in the United States

ISBN 978-1-4671-9854-7

Library of Congress Control Number: 2021943257

Notice: The information in this book is true and complete to the best of our knowledge. It is offered without guarantee on the part of the author or Arcadia Publishing. The author and Arcadia Publishing disclaim all liability in connection with the use of this book.

Produced by Shoreline Publishing Group LLC
Santa Barbara, California
Designer: Patty Kelley

Contents

WELCOME TO Memphis!

Look at a map of the United States and find the Mississippi River. It starts in Minnesota and flows south all the way to the Gulf of Mexico. One of the most important cities along that route is Memphis, Tennessee.

Located smack in the middle of the mid-South, Memphis is pretty much on the way to everywhere. The people are friendly and laid-back, and they love finding fun things to do, too.

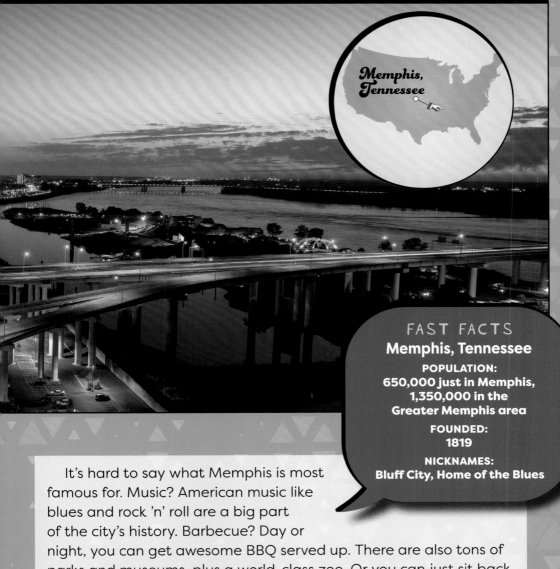

FAST FACTS
Memphis, Tennessee
POPULATION:
650,000 just in Memphis,
1,350,000 in the
Greater Memphis area
FOUNDED:
1819
NICKNAMES:
Bluff City, Home of the Blues

It's hard to say what Memphis is most famous for. Music? American music like blues and rock 'n' roll are a big part of the city's history. Barbecue? Day or night, you can get awesome BBQ served up. There are also tons of parks and museums, plus a world-class zoo. Or you can just sit back and gaze at the river!

In this book we'll find out what makes the Bluff City so great. Soon you'll be saying what murals across the city already do: "I love Memphis!"

MEMPHIS: Map It!

The larger metropolitan area of Memphis is actually in three states. Most of the city is in Tennessee. The southern part of the Greater Memphis area is actually in Mississippi (there, the town is called Southaven). And West Memphis jumps the state border (and the Mississippi River) into Arkansas. Don't worry—there are plenty of bridges to get you over there.

Memphis, Tennessee

KENTUCKY

MISSOURI

TENNESSEE

ARKANSAS

ALABAMA   GEORGIA

MISSISSIPPI

Memphis, Tennessee

ARKANSAS

TENNESSEE

Mississippi River

Mud Island

▲ Pyramid

Beale Street

National Civil Rights Museum

Graceland

MISSISSIPPI

N

City limits

Parks

– – – State borders

We're Not Bluffing!

To bluff means to fool someone. But in geography, a bluff is a cliff that overlooks water. And Memphis is famous for its bluffs.

The Chickasaw Bluffs run along the east coast of the Mississippi River in Tennessee. Memphis is located at the fourth bluff, which is the farthest to the south. That's how the city got its nickname, "Bluff City." The bluff helps protect the city in case the river floods, and it makes for pretty good lookout points, too!

Drink Up!

Memphis is known for drinking water that tastes fantastic. The city sits on top of a giant aquifer, which is like an underground lake with sand mixed in. Water has been collecting there for millions of years. Rainwater seeps down and is protected by a layer of clay, keeping it clean and pure. People drilled the first well into the aquifer in 1887. Since then, it's been Memphis's main source of water.

FAST FACT

The fourth Chickasaw Bluff was used as a stronghold by French soldiers in a 1739 battle against the Chickasaw people to control the region. The Chickasaw people were defending land that was already theirs, of course.

MEMPHiS MEANS . . .

Why the name Memphis? It comes from a much older city—Memphis, Egypt. When the founders of Memphis in Tennessee were looking for a name, they wanted to outdo the folks in Illinois who had recently named their city "Cairo," which is Egypt's capital city. So the Tennesseans picked Memphis, which means "beautiful place."

Memphis was the capital city of Ancient Egypt. It was located where the Great Pyramids of Giza stand today, on the large, powerful Nile River.

Memphis, Tennessee, has a large, powerful river, too. The mighty Mississippi River has always been an important part of the city's culture and economy. So the two Memphises have that in common. As for pyramids, well, the newer Memphis has one of those too!

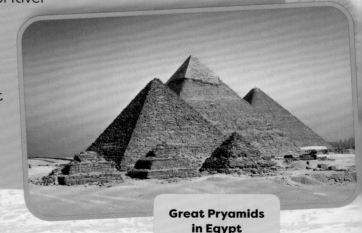

Great Pryamids in Egypt

Remains of ancient Memphis in Egypt

Today's Memphis has a huge pyramid, too. For more, turn the page!

WHAT'S YOUR POINT?

It's 321 feet tall (about 32 stories), and the base sides are 591 feet long.

Visitors can entertain themselves at an archery and shooting range, or visit the 600,000-gallon aquarium.

The freestanding elevator in the center is the tallest in the United States. There's transparent glass on all sides, so you better have a strong stomach if you take a ride to the top, where an observation deck overlooks the city.

The pyramids near the ancient city of Memphis, Egypt, were built thousands of years ago as tombs for royalty. But in the Memphis on *this* side of the Atlantic, there's just one pyramid. It was built in 1991. The idea wasn't to bury people there, but to make a giant sports and entertainment arena. That didn't work out, so in 2015 a Bass Pro Shop, an outdoor equipment and fishing gear store, moved in instead. The pyramid isn't quite as large as its Egyptian cousins, but it's still pretty impressive—and there are no mummies to deal with!

FAST FACT

The Memphis Pyramid had a crystal skull welded to the frame of the building, near the top. Some people say the skull cursed the pyramid, and that that was the reason it stayed empty for so long. Before BPS finally moved in, the pyramid was nicknamed "Tomb of Doom."

There's an indoor cypress swamp on the ground floor, complete with fish, alligators, and other swampy critters!

HISTORY: Early Days

People have lived along the Mississippi River for more than 10,000 years. About a thousand years ago, the powerful Mississippian culture developed around the area that is now Memphis. They were known for building huge mounds as tombs and for having agriculture based on maize, or corn. They thrived for the next 500 years. As they left the area, the Chickasaw from farther south on the Mississippi River took their place in the 1600s. They didn't have the place to themselves for long. European settlers arrived in the early 1700s.

The Mississippian civilization was a mound culture, groups of Native American peoples who built large mounds to use for burial grounds or other sacred purposes.

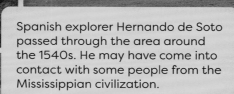

Spanish explorer Hernando de Soto passed through the area around the 1540s. He may have come into contact with some people from the Mississippian civilization.

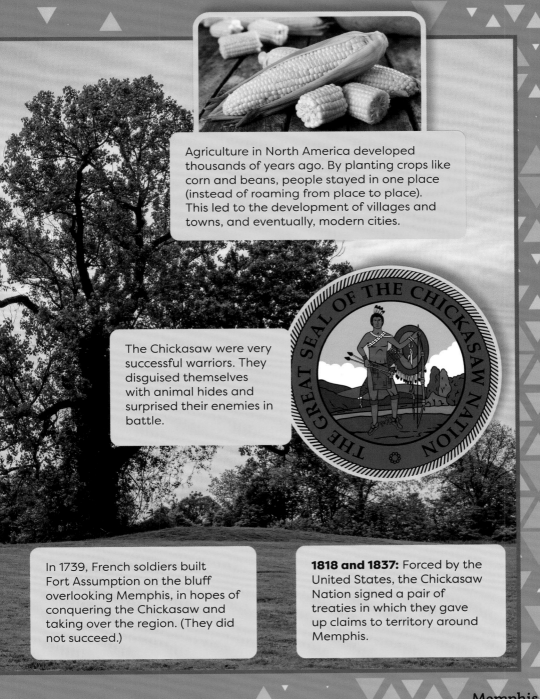

Agriculture in North America developed thousands of years ago. By planting crops like corn and beans, people stayed in one place (instead of roaming from place to place). This led to the development of villages and towns, and eventually, modern cities.

The Chickasaw were very successful warriors. They disguised themselves with animal hides and surprised their enemies in battle.

In 1739, French soldiers built Fort Assumption on the bluff overlooking Memphis, in hopes of conquering the Chickasaw and taking over the region. (They did not succeed.)

1818 and 1837: Forced by the United States, the Chickasaw Nation signed a pair of treaties in which they gave up claims to territory around Memphis.

HISTORY: Early Days

1819: The city of Memphis was founded by John Overton, James Winchester, and future president Andrew Jackson.

Andrew Jackson

John Overton

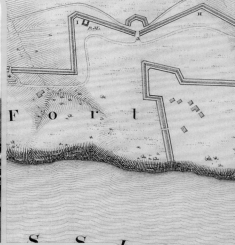

1857: The final rails were laid to finish the Memphis & Charleston Railroad. The tracks connected Memphis to the East Coast port of Charleston, South Carolina. It helped turn the city into an important transportation hub.

June 6, 1862: Tennessee was part of the Confederacy (the South) during the Civil War. On this day, Union (Northern) forces captured the city during the Battle of Memphis.

Fort Pickering was built on the bluffs over the Mississippi River by the Confederates, but was taken over and expanded in 1862 by Union forces.

1870s: Several yellow fever epidemics swept through the city in 1873, 1878, and 1879. Thousands of people died, and thousands more left the city.

1893: Black businessman Robert Church bought a $1,000 bond to help pay off the city's debt after a period of rebuilding expanded Memphis.

1916: In Memphis, Clarence Saunders founded the nation's first modern supermarket, the Piggly Wiggly. Customers walked up and down the aisles themselves to select their groceries, a new development in shopping at that time.

1930s: The Great Depression brought widespread hardship across America, but President Franklin D. Roosevelt had a plan, the "New Deal," to improve the economy. The powerful Memphis mayor Edward Crump made sure Memphis received money from the New Deal.

1942: The Army Corps of Engineers opened the Memphis General Depot. This large complex of buildings was used to store food, clothing, and equipment for soldiers during World War II. The depot even doubled as a camp to hold prisoners of war.

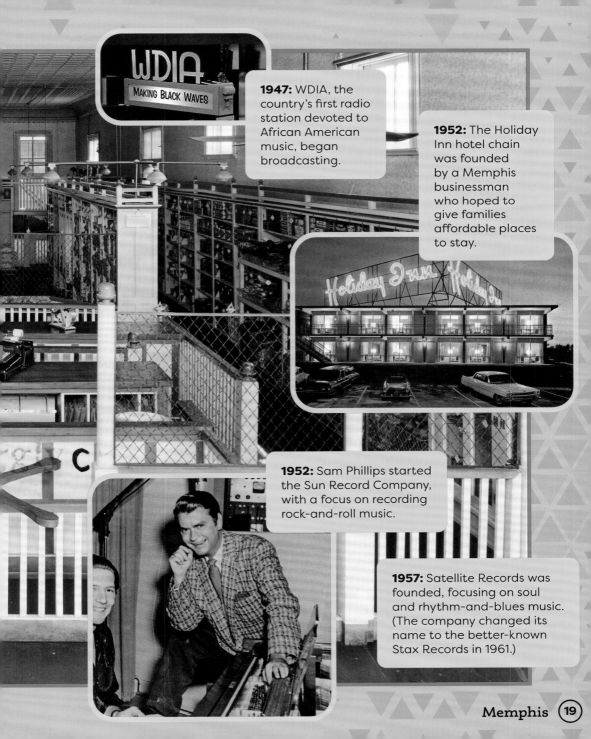

1947: WDIA, the country's first radio station devoted to African American music, began broadcasting.

1952: The Holiday Inn hotel chain was founded by a Memphis businessman who hoped to give families affordable places to stay.

1952: Sam Phillips started the Sun Record Company, with a focus on recording rock-and-roll music.

1957: Satellite Records was founded, focusing on soul and rhythm-and-blues music. (The company changed its name to the better-known Stax Records in 1961.)

The 1960s saw the battle for civil rights spread across the country, led by efforts in the South. The city of Memphis was at the heart of it.

October 3, 1961: Thirteen African American first-graders—the "Memphis 13"—went to four Memphis schools that used to allow only white students. This was the first time that any Memphis school was desegregated, or allowed Black and white students to learn together.

THE MEMPHIS 13
BRUCE ELEMENTARY SCHOOL

1966: Black sanitation workers protested unfair pay and dangerous working conditions by attempting to strike (or not work until conditions improved). They didn't get enough support, however, and nothing was done to improve conditions.

Surviving Memphis strikers met President Barack Obama in 2011.

February 1, 1968: Two Black sanitation workers were killed by a malfunctioning garbage truck.

February 12, 1968: In protest, 1,300 sanitation workers went on strike again. The strike continued for weeks, but Mayor Henry Loeb refused to make a deal for better pay and safer conditions.

April 4, 1968: The famous civil rights leader Dr. Martin Luther King, Jr., came to support the striking workers. When he stepped out for some fresh air on the balcony of his room at the Lorraine Motel, he was shot and killed by James Earl Ray, a white racist criminal. (See more on this story on page 48.)

HISTORY: Recent Times

1973: The shipping company Federal Express moved to Memphis.

1977: Elvis Presley died at his home, the Graceland mansion (see page 34).

1982: Graceland opened to the public as a museum.

1991: The Lorraine Motel re-opened as the National Civil Rights Museum (see page 48).

2001: Memphis got its first pro sports team when the NBA's Grizzlies moved to Memphis from Vancouver, British Columbia.

2003: A huge storm caused extensive damage all over Memphis. Locals called it "Hurricane Elvis."

2019: Memphis celebrated its bicentennial (its 200-year birthday).

People from the Past!

We could fill a book with amazing people from Memphis history. Here are some folks you might like meeting.

Ida B. Wells (1862-1931):
Civil rights activist Ida B. Wells lived in Memphis in the 1880s and 1890s. A Black woman, she worked as a teacher and then later ran a newspaper—something uncommon considering the time period she lived in. She was a fierce advocate for equality, and she became a national figure in the early fight for civil rights and equality for Black people.

Robert Church (1839-1912):
Born into slavery, Church later gained his freedom and became a businessman. He was so good at it that he became the South's first Black millionaire. He used some of his money to build a park and auditorium for Black Memphians.

Machine Gun Kelly (1895–1954):

His real name was George Kelly Barnes, but if you're going to be a gangster, you need something that sounds a little scarier! Kelly got his nickname from his favorite gun. After robbing banks and stores, he was finally arrested in 1933 in his hometown and sent to prison.

Edward "Boss" Crump (1874–1954):

Crump started his long political career in 1910, when he was elected mayor of Memphis. Later he served in the U.S. House of Representatives. He built a network of friends and contacts that gave him an enormous amount of power.

William Christopher (W.C.) Handy (1873–1958):

Known as the "Father of the Blues," Handy was a musician who actually helped get Boss Crump elected. He wrote Crump a campaign song called "Mr. Crump." Later the song title was changed to "Memphis Blues." Handy went on to write several more popular songs and became a regular Memphis performer.

MEMPHIS TODAY

Memphis started as a small town, but it's grown up and gotten famous in the last 200 years! Here are some things you'll definitely hear when the word "Memphis" is mentioned:

Music: Many great blues musicians have called Memphis home. That's why it's called the "Birthplace of the Blues." It's not just blues, either. There are also roots of soul, rhythm and blues, and of course, rock 'n' roll. Performers keep clubs around the city rockin'.

In and Out: Memphis is on the road to everywhere, from New Orleans to St. Louis to the west coast. It's an important inland port (one that isn't on the ocean), and its airport is the busiest in the world for cargo, thanks to being the hub of the global delivery company FedEx.

Civil Rights: Memphis remains at the heart of the continuing fight for equality. The city honors its civil rights history with museums, historic sites, events, and programs that promote social justice throughout the city and the nation.

SING OUT!
More than 1,000 songs mention Memphis in their lyrics—that's more than any other city in the world!

Barbecue: If there's one thing this city knows as well as its music, it's barbecue (especially pork). Locals and visitors both stay stuffed at the city's many barbecue joints.

MEMPHIS for Everyone

Memphis is a busy and diverse city. People from around the world have been coming to live here for two centuries! Today the city is home to families from across Central and South America, China, India, the Philippines, and other Asian nations. Much of Memphis's large Black population traces its roots to Africa, and there is a strong Sudanese community. Each year Memphis's diversity grows.

The Pinch

Immigrants from Ireland, Greece, and Russia arrived in Memphis in the 1800s. They settled in the Pinch, one of the city's first neighborhoods and commercial districts. After World War II, residents began leaving the area to live in newly built suburbs, and the Pinch suffered economically. Now, however, local businesses and people are starting to move back into this historic community. It is also home to St. Jude Children's Hospital.

Orange Mound

In 1890, a white developer named Izey Meacham bought a former plantation in Memphis called Orange Mound. He divided the land into small plots. He sold them for about $100 each to African American families. It was the first neighborhood in the United States meant specifically for the African American community. The new residents built homes, schools, churches, and businesses in Orange Mound. It remains a strong community in Memphis.

Latinx Population

Latinx immigrants have established strong roots in Memphis. People from Latin countries make up about six percent of the city's population. Most are from Mexico, although there are people from countries across Central and South America. A boom in Latinx immigration began in the 1990s. By 2000 the city's Latinx population had more than tripled! Today most Latinx Memphians are young people building community in neighborhoods like Hickory Hill, Nutbush, and Berclair where Latinx culture thrives in neighborhood restaurants and shops.

Italian Influence

In the early 1800s, European immigrants came to America to escape poor economic and social conditions. Over the next century, millions of people arrived in the United States. The first Italian immigrants came to Memphis in about 1836. In fact, only the city of New Orleans welcomed more people from Italy in those early years. Italian immigrants built their own communities in Memphis— and they're still thriving.

And Everywhere Else!

Memphis has something for everyone, maybe because there's a little bit of everyone there! People from more than 50 countries live in Memphis, including Vietnam, Nigeria, India, Ethiopia, and South Korea. Neighborhoods like Binghampton and the Heights are some of the most ethnically diverse in the city.

ticky Situation
Memphis Climate and Weather

Really, it's the humidity: Climate people use words like "humid subtropical" and "moist continental" when they talk about Memphis. Those are fancy ways of saying that Memphis can be pretty sticky, especially in the summer. Memphians call it "muggy."

It's Sunny! Memphis has more sunny days than most places in the United States. The city averages 218 sunny days each year—more than the national average.

A four-season place: The good news is the city sees four distinct seasons. The temperature usually doesn't climb out of the 90s in the summer, or sink below freezing in the winter.

Actually, five seasons: Early spring, and sometimes late fall, is when the city gets its "severe weather season." Cold air seeps in from Canada, and warm air drifts up from the Gulf of Mexico. When the two meet, they cause weather conditions that can bring thunderstorms, hail, and tornadoes.

What's that white stuff? Memphis gets the occasional snowstorm, but don't hold your breath waiting for a snow day. Most winters see only about 3 inches of snowfall.

Best times to visit: Weather-wise, the city is nicest during April and May, and then again in October. The summer is hotter and a lot more humid.

ELVIS
AARON
PRESLEY

JANUARY 8, 1935
AUGUST 16, 1977

SON OF
VERNON ELVIS PRESLEY
AND
GLADYS LOVE PRESLEY
FATHER OF
LISA MARIE PRESLEY

HE WAS A PRECIOUS GIFT FROM GOD
WE CHERISHED AND LOVED DEARLY.
HE HAD A GOD-GIVEN TALENT THAT HE S
WITH THE WORLD, AND WITHOUT A DOUB
HE BECAME MOST WIDELY ACCLAIMED;
CAPTURING THE HEARTS OF YOUNG AND
HE WAS ADMIRED NOT ONLY AS AN ENT
BUT AS THE GREAT HUMANITARIAN THA
FOR HIS GENEROSITY, AND HIS KIND FEE
FOR HIS FELLOW MAN.
HE REVOLUTIONIZED THE FIELD OF MUSI
RECEIVED ITS HIGHEST AWARDS.
HE BECAME A LIVING LEGEND IN HIS O
EARNING THE RESPECT AND LOVE OF M
GOD SAW THAT HE NEEDED SOME REST
CALLED HIM HOME TO BE WITH HIM.
WE MISS YOU, SON AND DADDY. I THA
THAT HE GAVE US YOU AS OUR SON.

Things to see in Memphis

If it's your first time in Memphis, these are some cool places to check out:

Graceland

Rock 'n' roll legend Elvis Presley bought Graceland, a Memphis mansion, in 1957. In addition to all the normal rooms, there was a music room (of course) and a pool room (for a pool table, not swimming). One room was decorated with a tropical theme and even had a waterfall. Elvis called it "the den" and liked to relax there. Now it's known as the "Jungle Room." After Elvis died, his widow, Priscilla, turned the house into a museum. Now visitors can see all of Elvis's stuff—from clothing to cars to fancy guitars—and buy souvenirs on their way out.

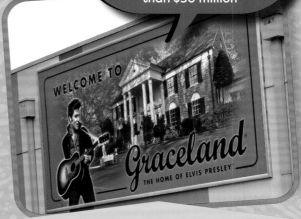

GRACELAND
NUMBERS:
17,552 square feet
23 rooms
13.8-acre property
Cost to buy: $102,500
Estimated value now: more than $50 million

Long Live the King: Elvis combined the sound of the blues with the "new" sound of rock in the 1950s. His outlandish performing style and good looks made him a national star. He made dozens of albums, and was known as the "King of Rock 'n' Roll." Elvis died in 1977, when he was just 42.

Beale Street

MEMPHIS'S TOURIST PLAYGROUND

The Memphis music scene all started on Beale Street, beginning when the African American community started growing in the 1800s. By the 1920s, it was the go-to place for dozens of famous blues and jazz musicians. Beale Street saw some hard times in the 1960s and 1970s, but the city worked hard to bring it back. Now, musicians play the clubs, and tourists (and locals) pack the street every day of the week. Beale Street is just under two miles long, but there's a lot to see along the way. Don't miss these places:

FAST FACT
Famous musicians like B.B. King, Muddy Waters, and Louis Armstrong all performed on Beale Street.

A. Schwab's: Need some pickles? A new hat? A ukelele? It's all under one roof at A. Schwab, a general store that got its start back in 1876.

W.C. Handy Home and Museum: The Memphis house where blues legend William Christopher (W.C.) Handy lived in the early 1900s was moved to Beale and 4th Street in the 1980s. He wrote a popular song called "Beale Street Blues." Before that, the street was actually called Beale Avenue. Handy's song was so popular the street was renamed to match the song!

Memphis Rock 'n' Soul Museum: Get the full story on Memphis music, from the blues to rock. There are tons of exhibits about Memphis-influenced artists and the city's radio stations and recording studios. Plus, you'll get to listen to lots of music with the audio tour, so you can hear how things changed over the years.

Victorian Village

There's no place like home—
especially the homes of
wealthy Memphis families
in the late 1800s. Victorian
Village is a cluster of fancy
mansions that have seen a
lot of history over the years.

Overton Square

If you get tired of playing in Memphis's famous—and large!—Overton
Park (page 80), head south a block. At Overton Square you can grab
some food and wander around to see the art and maybe catch a
concert at the Hattiloo Theatre. Nearby Overton Park is also home to
an outdoor theater, the Levitt Shell.

Crosstown Concourse

This enormous building is over a million square feet. It was originally a warehouse and office building for the Sears department store. When Sears moved out, no one moved in for two decades. It finally got a makeover in 2017. Now it's filled with shops, restaurants, offices, and even apartments. Basically, once you go in you never need to come back out—unless you want to discover more cool places in Memphis!

Duck, Duck, More Ducks

At the Peabody Hotel, the most famous occupants actually live there full-time—on the roof! They are a group of five ducks—one drake (a male) and four hens (female). Each morning at 11 o'clock they ride down the elevator, waddle across a red carpet, and spend the next six hours splashing around in the hotel's lobby fountain. At 5 o'clock they go back up the elevator to spend the evening in their rooftop "Royal Duck Palace." (There's a fountain up there, too.) The event started as a joke in the 1920s, but is now a Memphis tradition.

New ducks are trained in this important business every three months, and the retired ducks go to a farm to live out their days. A "duckmaster" takes care of the fowl while they're at the Peabody, making sure no one "ducks" out on their duties!

The Mighty Mississippi

How long does it take to stroll down the Lower Mississippi River, from Cairo, Illinois to its dumping point into the Gulf of Mexico, south of New Orleans? About an hour. That is, if you're walking (and sometimes wading) on the Riverwalk. This scale model of the Big Muddy (that's a nickname for the river) at Mud Island River Park covers 1,000 miles of river in 2,000 feet. It's made of cement (and water, of course) to show the topography (the landscape) of the real river and landmarks along the way.

Mississippi River Info

At 2,350 miles long, the "Mighty Missisipp" is America's second longest river (behind the Missouri) and by far its most important. For thousands of years, it was the "highway" for people from north to south. Indigenous people settled around it and used it to reach distant lands. When Europeans arrived, it was the way many of them reached the far west. It remains a key part of the national transportation network.

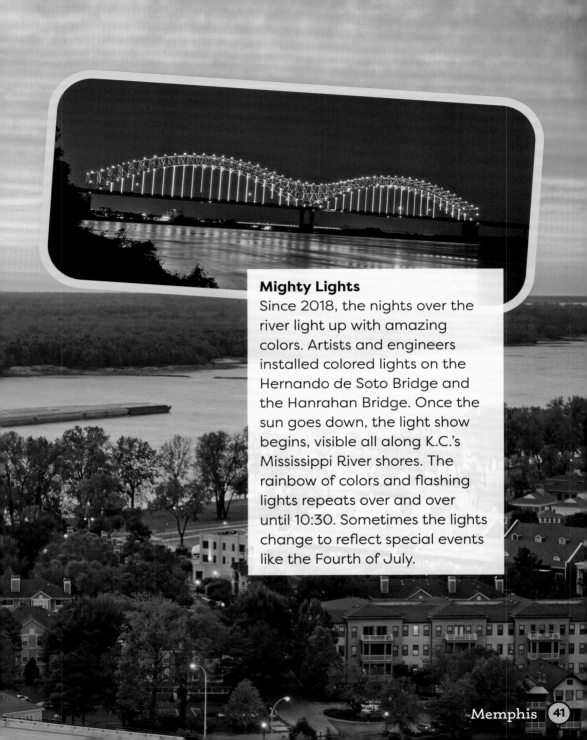

Mighty Lights

Since 2018, the nights over the river light up with amazing colors. Artists and engineers installed colored lights on the Hernando de Soto Bridge and the Hanrahan Bridge. Once the sun goes down, the light show begins, visible all along K.C.'s Mississippi River shores. The rainbow of colors and flashing lights repeats over and over until 10:30. Sometimes the lights change to reflect special events like the Fourth of July.

GETTING AROUND

MEMPHIS

Memphis is fairly spread out, so you'll want to know your options for getting from one place to another. There's a bus system, but that's best if you're not in a hurry and don't mind taking some detours. Here are some other options:

Car Culture:
Most people get around by car. You can use your own, or your family can rent one. That's probably the fastest and easiest way to get to places that aren't right in the city center. And of course, you can always call a taxi or a ride-sharing service for a quick hop from here to there.

Take to the Trolleys

In the 1800s, Memphians got around on streetcars, which were electric trolleys that ran on rails in the middle of the streets. The original system closed down in 1947, but some new lines opened in the 1990s. The Main Street Line remains today as a great way to take a trip to the past . . . in the present!

Bike Share

If you're up for a little exercise, try renting a bike through the city's bike share system. Hundreds of bikes are available at about 80 stations all over the city. If you're not up for a little exercise, you can also rent an electric bike and save some energy!

On the Water

Stand on the deck of an old-fashioned paddlewheel riverboat and get an idea of what it was like when riverboats were seen up and down the Mississippi. Yes, you're going to end up in the same place you left from, but it's still a fun way to see the city.

IT'S OFFICIAL!

Hey, that's ours! Cities and states like to pick their favorite things. They tell everyone about it by making it "official." Here's some stuff from Memphis and Tennessee:

OFFICIAL CITY FLOWER:
crepe myrtle (which is actually a shrub)

OFFICIAL CITY MOTTO:
"The City of Good Abode" (Abode = place to live)

OFFICIAL CITY FLAG:
The three colored sections in the Memphis flag represent the three states that Memphis covers: red for Tennessee, blue for Mississippi, and white for Arkansas.

OFFICIAL TENNESSEE STATE STUFF

Bird: Mockingbird

Butterfly: Zebra Swallowtail

Beverage: Milk

Fruit: Tomato

Fossil: Pterotrigonia
(a small water animal with a shell)

Rock: Limestone

Horse: Tennessee Walking Horse

Amphibian:
Tennessee Cave Salamander

OFFICIAL CITY TREE:
dogwood

What a Ride! Artist Tylur French used 320 old bicycles to create the bike arch on the east side of Overton Park. They're all painted bright colors and welded to a steel frame. The whole thing weighs about 7,000 pounds. The sculpture has become a meeting place for the city's cyclists. Pretty good way to re-cycle, huh?

Art in Memphis

Outdoor Art

Outside art can be found all over Memphis!

Broad Avenue Arts District: Here you'll find lots of galleries and boutiques with paintings, sculptures, crafts, and jewelry. But if you prefer to stay outside, that works, too. The Broad Avenue district has one of Memphis's largest murals, as well as its highest—it's on the side of a tall water tower. Heck, even the bus stop is artistic!

More than Like: Memphis artists are pretty clear on how they feel about their city. All around town, muralists have painted "I Love Memphis" murals in all kinds of different styles. See how many you spot!

I AM A MAN Plaza: The giant capital letters that state "I AM A MAN" are the focal point in this park. It's a tribute to the Black workers from the city's sanitation strike in 1968. They carried signs with these words.

I AM A MAN Plaza was commissioned by the City of

Great Museums!

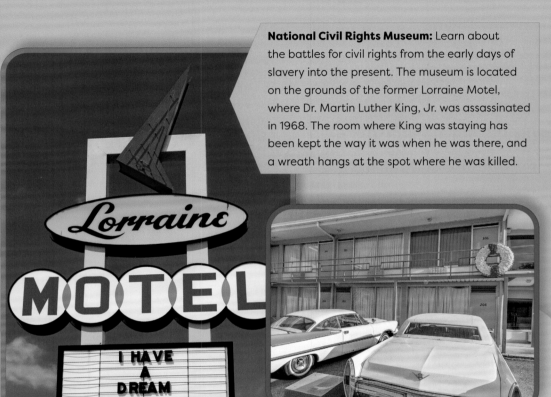

National Civil Rights Museum: Learn about the battles for civil rights from the early days of slavery into the present. The museum is located on the grounds of the former Lorraine Motel, where Dr. Martin Luther King, Jr. was assassinated in 1968. The room where King was staying has been kept the way it was when he was there, and a wreath hangs at the spot where he was killed.

Lorraine
MOTEL
I HAVE A DREAM MLK

A statue honors Rosa Parks, whose refusal to give up her seat to a white bus rider in Alabama in 1955 helped spark the Civil Rights Movement.

Sun Studio: Elvis famously made his first recording here for $4. It was a gift for his mother. Soon he was the country's most famous star, and Sun Studio went on to become a legend in rock 'n' roll recording. Tours are available of the studio, which is still in business, although it'll cost you more than $4 to rent space now.

Stax Museum of American Soul Music: Travel back to the early 20th century to find the roots of Memphis soul music. The Stax Museum has original instruments and equipment used by the studio's first artists, as well as photos, costumes and other memorabilia. Films and recordings round out the experience. And if you can't stay still while listening to all the great music, there's even a dance floor!

Great Museums!

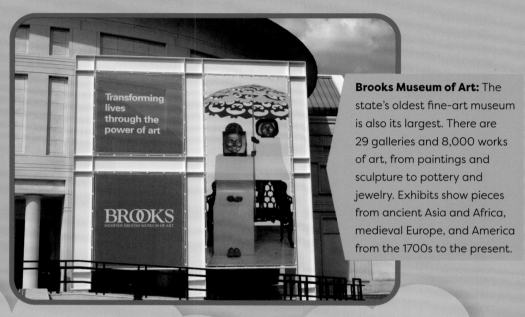

Brooks Museum of Art: The state's oldest fine-art museum is also its largest. There are 29 galleries and 8,000 works of art, from paintings and sculpture to pottery and jewelry. Exhibits show pieces from ancient Asia and Africa, medieval Europe, and America from the 1700s to the present.

The Dixon Gallery and Gardens: The Dixon Gallery makes a good first impression—and second and third, too. It's full of works by famous French impressionists, a style of art that was popular in the late 1800s. And when you're ready to come up (and go out) for air, take a walk in the 17 acres of gardens.

Metal Museum: Gold, silver, iron—if it's made of metal, it's got a home here. Metal objects of every kind are the focus of this museum, with more than 3,000 pieces of sculpture, jewelry, and decorative items. The museum also runs a studio for artists.

Pink Palace: Clarence Saunders, who founded the grocery store Piggly Wiggly, began building this huge mansion out of pink marble back in the 1920s. When he ran out of money, the city took it over. Now it's the Museum of Science & History, with information on the region's history, cool science exhibits on everything from dinosaurs to medical breakthroughs, a 65-acre nature center, a planetarium, and a huge theater.

See the World in Memphis

Memphians are devoted to diversity. Check out these places that celebrate cultures from all over the world.

◄ The **Belz Museum of Asian and Judaic Art** holds more than 1,000 items! It includes one of the largest collections from China's Q'ing dynasty (which was in power from 1644 to 1912). There's also a focus on Jewish artists, with a special tribute to Holocaust survivors.

➤ Visitors to the **Slave Haven Underground Railroad Museum** literally go underground, through trap doors that lead to a cellar. That's because the house used to be a stop on the Underground Railroad. It wasn't actually a railroad, but a series of safe places where enslaved people hid on their way North to freedom.

◄ Go back more than 1,000 years to the home of ancient people at the **Chucalissa Archaeological Site** in T.O. Fuller State Park. The Mississippian civilization lived there from about the years 1000-1500. Now there's a museum, and a lab to train archaeologists.

Nigerian artist Ephraim Urevbu runs **Urevbu Contemporary**, an art gallery that's devoted to showing works by African artists and celebrating diversity in the arts.

Performing Arts

It's not just Beale Street. Memphis has tons of cool places for the performing arts!

Ballet Memphis is proud of its diverse and talented dancers and programs.

The historic Orpheum Theatre has been going strong since 1928. It's one of Memphis's best spots for live music and stage shows.

The **Cannon Center** can seat more than 2,000 people and is the home of the Memphis Symphony Orchestra.

Go old-school and see a flick at the **Malco Summer Drive-In** movie theater, where they show both current and classic movies. It's got a cool '50s vibe and you pay by the car, not per person. That's a bargain if you go with a lot of friends!

How to Talk Memphis

If you go somewhere new, you'll need to know what the locals are talking about. Here's how they say things in "M-town":

'Cue

Take a "cue" from the locals and don't bother to say the whole word for "barbecue."

Old and New

Two major bridges crossing the Mississippi River are called the Memphis & Arkansas Bridge and the Hernando de Soto Bridge. That's a lot to remember, so folks just call them the "Old Bridge" (for the Memphis & Arkansas) and the "New Bridge" (for the Hernando de Soto).

I Believe

Memphians have faith in the Grizzlies, and t-shirts and caps with the "I Believe" slogan are how they show their support for the team.

Beale Street Bears

The Forum is located just off Beale Street, so fans sometimes use this nickname for the team.

MEMPHIS: It's Weird!

Crystal Shrine Grotto

Mexican sculptor Dionicio Rodriguez created this grotto (cave) in Memorial Park Cemetery in the 1930s. He decorated it with cement stalactites (the formations that hang from the ceiling) and quartz crystals. Then he added religious figurines and pictures to give it a spiritual feel. The whole thing is lit up with colored lights, and harp music plays on a sound system.

Goat to It!?

At Silky O'Sullivan's pub on Beale Street, visitors can feed the pair of goats that live there. A tower at the restaurant has a circular ramp built around it that the goats like to climb. Hey, it keeps the goats—and the guests—entertained!

Vote for Mongo!

Don't worry if you're not old enough to vote yet. Prince Mongo (real name: Robert Hodges) has been running for mayor of Memphis since 1978. He'll probably still be at it for years to come—even though he hasn't won yet. Mongo/Hodges says he's more than 300 years old and comes from the planet Zambodia. Maybe he should try running in his home galaxy?

Weird Memphis Laws

You don't want to get on the wrong side of the law when you're in Memphis. These weird laws were once on the books. Good thing they're not enforced anymore!
• It was illegal for a woman to drive unless a man walked in front of her car, waving a red flag to warn anyone who might be in the way.
• It was illegal for frogs to croak after 11 p.m.
• It was illegal to take leftover pie home from a restaurant. Plus, you couldn't give it to anyone else to finish up for you.

Meet Marvelous Memphians!

Morgan Freeman

Born in Memphis: June 1, 1937

Freeman is an award-winning actor known for powerful roles and his booming voice. He's starred in dozens of movies including the Batman Dark Knight trilogy and The LEGO movie. After high school, he joined the Air Force to become a fighter pilot, but he soon realized that he liked acting better!

Justin Timberlake

Born in Memphis: January 31, 1981

Timberlake started his career as a professional singer in the pop band *NSYNC. He went solo in 2002, and won several Grammy Awards. Now he's one of the bestselling pop singers ever! Timberlake also has started several businesses, and does a lot of charity work that helps children and fights hunger.

What People Do
IN MEMPHIS

With more than a million people living in and around Memphis, there's a lot to do to keep the city running. Here's a look at where people work and some of the things they do all day (and night!):

The International Port of Memphis just south of Downtown stretches for 15 miles along the banks of the Mississippi River. Along that route are 37 terminals that carry cargo such as oil, coal, salt, rock, grain, and cement.

Put it on a plane! The Memphis airport is the busiest in the world for cargo. That's in large part because of Federal Express, which started here in 1971. FedEx's huge airport operation is called "the matrix." As big as more than 600 football fields put together, it even has its own fire department and police force!

memphis is headquarters for International Paper, one of the world's largest companies for making paper, pulp, and packaging products. That means stuff like sacks, boxes, envelopes, and printer paper.

Health care is big business in memphis. There are several major hospitals and a research center through the university of Tennessee. The city also has a number of companies that make important medical devices like pacemakers and replacement joints.

AutoZone is a nationwide chain with more than 6,000 stores selling auto parts and accessories. The original business was actually a grocery store called malone & Hyde, but the company's president decided in 1979 to branch out. Good move!

Agribusiness is just what it sounds like—the business of agriculture. memphis companies process soybeans, meat, and lots of other foods. Processing cotton is also still a big part of the memphis economy. Forty percent of the country's cotton crop goes through the city.

Eat the Memphis Way

If it tastes good, you can find it in Memphis—just be ready to leave with a full stomach!

Barbecue No other city is as famous as Memphis for barbecue—especially pork. You can get it the traditional way, with a side of cornbread and some greens, but Memphians love their 'cue so much that they also put it on top of nachos, pizza, and spaghetti.

Wet or dry? That's the big question when it comes to barbecue. Be prepared to decide whether you want "wet," which is basted while it's cooking and served with sauce, or "dry," which is rubbed with spices before cooking and served sauceless.

Family recipes are the basis for **Gus's World Famous Fried Chicken**. The restaurant now has dozens of locations across the United States, but it all started here.

Secret Ingredient

Get a taste of history with a deep-fried hamburger at Dyer's Burgers, where burgers are cooked in the same batch of grease the restaurant started with back in 1912. (They add new grease when it runs low.) The restaurant takes its grease very seriously. When they moved to a new location, they hired an armed guard to get the grease there safely.

FAST FACT
Soybeans are Tennessee's biggest crop, with almost a billion dollars a year in sales.

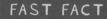

Memphians know how to make dessert, too. At **Jerry's Snow Cones**, they serve up flavored ice with vanilla ice cream on top.

Gibson's Donuts has perfected the glazed donut, but they've branched out into other tasty treats as well. Try the maple bacon donut if you can't decide whether you want sweet or salty—get both!

Go, Memphis Sports!

What's your favorite sport? Memphians have lots of teams to choose from—and they're *fan*atical about cheering them on!

MEMPHIS GRIZZLIES

Joined the National Basketball Association in 1995 as the Vancouver Grizzlies, and moved to Memphis in 2001.

Known for their "grit and grind" style, using pressure on the ball to create tough defense

Famous for the mascot named Grizz, who entertains fans during games

Big Names: Mike Conley, Zach Randolph, Ja Morant, Marc Gasol, Pau Gasol

Home: FedEx Forum

From 1970 to 1975 Memphis had another pro basketball team. It was part of the American Basketball Association. The team changed names three times. First they were the Memphis Pros, then the Memphis Tams, and finally the Memphis Sounds.

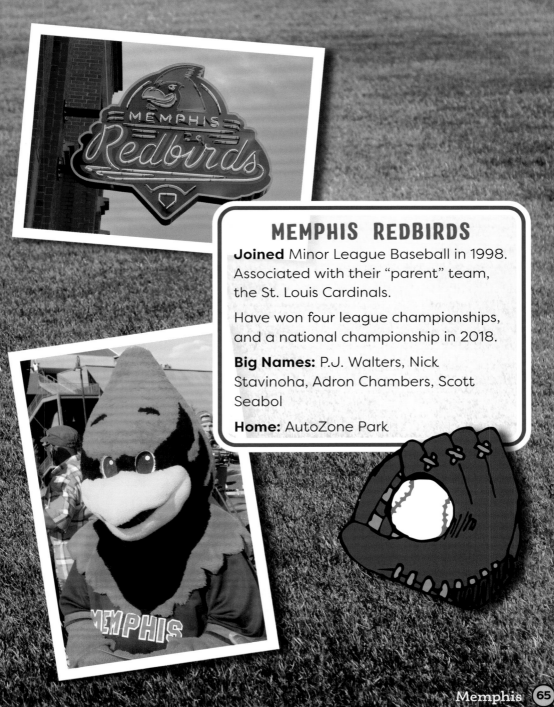

MEMPHIS REDBIRDS

Joined Minor League Baseball in 1998. Associated with their "parent" team, the St. Louis Cardinals.

Have won four league championships, and a national championship in 2018.

Big Names: P.J. Walters, Nick Stavinoha, Adron Chambers, Scott Seabol

Home: AutoZone Park

MEMPHIS 901

Joined the United Soccer League in 2018.

What's the 901 for? Hint: Think about it, and you'll probably "call" it correctly!

Big Names: Kyle Murphy, Kadeem Dacres, Laurent Kissiedou

Home: AutoZone Park

GO, TIGERS, GO!

Besides its pro teams, Memphians rally around their college athletes, too. The University of Memphis Tigers compete in Division I of the NCAA. That's the toughest level of college sports. U of M has teams in basketball, football, baseball, soccer, golf, and even rifle shooting. The college's men's basketball team has been particularly successful, often reaching the NCAA tournament.

FAST FACT

For years, the university had a mascot of a live Bengal tiger named TOM (which stands for "Tigers of Memphis"). When the most recent tiger, TOM III, died in 2020, the university decided not to bring live animals to games anymore. Instead, they decided to sponsor a tiger at the Memphis Zoo. He'll attend games via a webcam.

Other Sports!

Memphis has something for everyone!

Cyclingl There are more than 60 miles of bike paths and trails in Memphis, some paved and some not. Many go through the city's parks. Check out the Hampline, a quick two-mile ride on a bike-and-pedestrian way that links Overton Park with the Broad Avenue Arts District.

Let's Roll The Memphis Roller Derby started in 2006 and has about 30 volunteer skaters. Officially the team is a member of the Women's Flat Track Derby Association, but men are welcome to join, too!

Golf Memphians love their golf! There are more than 30 golf courses in the city and surrounding area. The city is also a regular site for pro events like the PGA's World Golf Championship and the LPGA's Pink Ribbon Open.

The Races Are On Hundreds of citizens turn out for St. Jude Children's Research Hospital's annual marathon to raise money. There is a full marathon (26.2 miles), plus a half-marathon, a 10K, and a 5K.

If running's not your thing, the hospital also sponsors an annual dragon boat race for 300 meters on the Mississippi River. The entry fee covers a team of 20 people and includes training and renting the 42-foot long boats. Afterward, there's music and food.

COLLEGE TOWN

Whether you want a big college campus or a cozy little school, Memphis has lots of places to get smart!

UNIVERSITY OF MEMPHIS

Founded 1912
Students: 21,000
Popular majors: health and physical education, nursing, psychology, business and management

THE UNIVERSITY OF MEMPHIS®

Fast Fact: The college changed its name from "Memphis State University" in 1994, but lots of people still use the old name.

Rudi E. Scheidt School of Music

RHODES COLLEGE

Founded 1848 (moved to Memphis in 1925)
Students: 2,000
Popular majors: business and management, biology, computer science, political science
Fast Fact: Students run a newspaper called *The Bridge* that helps provide jobs to people experiencing homelessness.

CHRISTIAN BROTHERS UNIVERSITY

Founded 1871
Students: 1,600
Popular majors: engineering, business and management, psychology, natural sciences
Fast Fact: It's the oldest college in Memphis—the first graduate was in 1875.

SOUTHWEST TENNESSEE COMMUNITY COLLEGE

Founded 2000
Students: 4,500
Popular majors: liberal arts, health professions, business
Fast Fact: The college formed when Shelby State and Southwest Technical Institute merged into one school.

LEMOYNE-OWEN COLLEGE

Founded 1924
Students: 800
Popular majors: business and management, liberal arts, criminal justice, biology
Fast Fact: Started in 1862 as an elementary school, today it's Memphis's only historically Black college (HBC).

LOL!
Did You Hear the One About?

Go ahead and laugh at Memphis—its people won't mind! Here are some riddles to tickle your funny bone.

Why is Memphis a solid place to live?

It's built on rock.

What happens when you call Memphis, Tennesee by its initials?

It becomes MT!

What did the Memphians say as the river flowed south?

I'll Mississippi you!

Why are there no yellow houses in Memphis?

They prefer blues.

What happens during the annual barbecue competition in Memphis?

Everyone goes hog wild.

Why do the Memphis Grizzlies try so hard to win basketball games?

They can't BEAR to lose!

Why does cotton have trouble making friends?

It's always bale-ing on them.

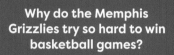

Why did Elvis Presley spend 20 years in Graceland?

It was his house!

Why is the Mississippi River the most famous in America?

It's the mudder of them all.

City

It's Alive! Animals in Memphis

Do you feel like you're being watched? Memphis is packed with wildlife of all kinds. They live in trees, parks, and backyards. Take a minute to look around and see what's got eyes on you!

Great horned owl

Fox

Red-tailed hawk

Coyote

Opossum

Where the Buffalo, er, Bison Roam

Wild bison (the official name for what some call buffalo) used to cover the prairies of the United States. Native peoples

depended on them for food and fur. American settlers, however, hunted them to near extinction. Today, parks and shelters are trying to protect the animals. In Memphis, Shelby Farms Park is home to 15 bison.

It's Alive! Animals in Memphis

With rivers all around the city, the term "wet and wild" gets a whole new meaning in Memphis. These animals live in the water and surrounding wetlands:

Beaver

River otter

Water moccasin
(cottonmouth snake)

Bald eagle

Darter

New Arrivals

Tennessee isn't as hot and swampy as states farther south, but alligators still find it comfortable enough to make this state their home. These large reptiles have been moving north into the area for several years. If the weather turns cold, the alligators can take it. In partly frozen water, they stick their snouts above the ice while the rest of them "chills out" below.

WE SAW IT AT THE ZOO

The Memphis Zoo got its start back in 1904. Memphis's old baseball team, the Turtles, had a mascot that was a bear (don't ask why). "Natch" the bear lived in Overton Park, where he spent his days chained to a tree. Other animals soon got dropped off in the park, too. The city finally decided to build them all an official home. Now the zoo has more than 4,500 animals!

It's panda-monium inside the Memphis Zoo. Pandas are their big thing. Actually, their giant thing. This zoo is one of the few in the United States that is home to a pair of giant pandas, Ya Ya and Le Le.

Giant panda

Navigate the Northwest Passage to see polar bears and sea lions. Because they spend a lot of their time underwater, these fuzzy creatures' exhibits are complete with a window below the waterline, so you can view them anytime!

Polar bear

Meercat

Giraffe

Grizzly bear

Take the Teton Trek for a look at animals that are native to Yellowstone National Park in Wyoming. Here you'll find grizzly bears, wolves, elk and all kinds of birds.

Park It Here

Memphis has some great parks. Here are some of Memphians' favorite places to go and get some fresh air:

Shelby Farms is a huge park with miles of trails, ponds, and fun playgrounds. There is even a water park! You can even ride a bike there on the Greenline, which links the park to the center of the city. Keep an eye out for the bison herd that lives there too.

Overton Park, in the middle of the city, has the Memphis Zoo, a golf course, and a merry-go-round. Plus, there's lots of open space to play or walk around and look at the park's many pieces of outdoor sculpture. Be sure to take a walk through the Old Forest. Some of the trees there are more than 100 years old!

Named for a Black riverboat captain who saved dozens of people in a 1925 accident, **Tom Lee Park** on the Mississippi River will be packed with fun. City planners are adding more play areas, native plants, and picnic areas to make it one of Memphis's "go-to" spots.

Any kid can have fun at **Riverdale Park**, just outside Memphis in Germantown. The park is wheelchair-accessible. There's a huge treehouse with swings and gliders, plus a rink for street hockey, tennis courts, and a batting cage.

Spooky Sights

Some people believe in ghosts, some don't. Whatever your opinion, it's still fun to visit these places where ghosts are said to hang around. Their stories are definitely alive and well!

In the 1870s, the **Woodruff-Fontaine House** in Victorian Village was the home of Amos Woodruff and his family, including his daughter Mollie. She had a sad life, with both her son and her husband dying young. Mollie must miss them. Visitors say they sometimes see her sitting on her bed, and can smell her perfume in the air.

In 1918, a police officer named **Edward Broadfoot** was chasing bootleggers (people who sold alcohol illegally). He faced off with them at a cafe at 546 Main St., where one of the suspects shot and killed him. People say that Broadfoot is still afoot, patrolling the location a century later.

Across the street from Officer Broadfoot's last stand, you can grab a burger at **Earnestine and Hazel's**. There's usually plenty of company, from living customers to the ghosts of people who have come through the door over the years. The jukebox is especially haunted: it will randomly start playing songs—even when it's not plugged in!

This seat's taken—Seat C5 at the **Orpheum Theatre**, that is. It's reserved for Mary, a 12-year-old girl who was hit by a trolley outside the theater in 1921. Maybe Mary needed something to do in the afterlife, because now she hangs around the theater, slamming doors and turning the lights on and off. Sometimes she goes on stage to perform, too!

One afternoon in 1884, ten-year-old Claude Pugh was playing with a toy boat, when he fell into **Hebe Fountain** in Court Square and drowned. Now his ghost is said to appear near the fountain where he occasionally plays with new generations of kids who stop by his "haunt."

MEMPHIS BY THE NUMBERS

Stats and facts and digits . . . galore! Here are some of the numbers that make Memphis what it is.

6,540
Miles from Memphis, Tennessee to the site of the ancient Memphis, Egypt

430 feet
Height of the tallest building in Memphis, located at 100 North Main Street.

12 million*
Annual Visitors
*And growing!

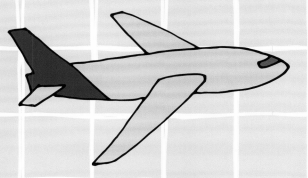

100+

Number of barbecue restaurants

1.5 Million

Number of FedEx packages that go through Memphis each *day*

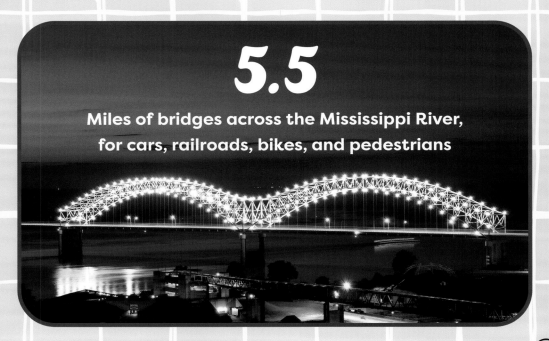

5.5

Miles of bridges across the Mississippi River, for cars, railroads, bikes, and pedestrians

Not Far Away

It's not likely you'll run out of things to do in Memphis, but you can find plenty to do on your way in or out of town, too. Check out these places nearby:

Hey! Where you been?

We went camping on the **Wolf River**!

I thought you were in Memphis…?

Wolf River flows into Memphis from Mississippi. Not as big as THE river, but still more than 100 miles long. It was formed when glaciers melted!

Glaciers? In the South?

Old ones LOL. That was 12,000 years ago.

Did you fish?

Nope, but saw some cool animals—deer, an eagle, a couple of otters. Pretty sure I saw a bobcat, too.

OK, *now* we went fishing.

Fishing for trees?

That's what makes **Reelfoot Lake** so cool. It was formed 15,000 years ago by an earthquake. Now those cypress trees grow in it. But there are fish, too.

I guess it's the *reel* thing.

😊 Leaving now.

Back on land finally!

Where to now?

Tupelo, Mississippi. Just down the road from Memphis. It's where Elvis was born. You can see his original house.

Is it as fancy as Graceland?

Not so much. Only two rooms here—not 23! ! But it's still cool to see where the King's journey began!

Check this out!

Quite a hill.

It's not a HILL, it's a MOUND.

Um, there's a difference?

Big one. This is at **Pinson Mounds State Archaeological Park**. There are about 15 mounds that were built by ancient people.

What for?

Some were burial places. But there are others with flat tops, where people could gather. Those were probably used for seasonal ceremonies.

Could you climb them?

Yup! Plus there's loads of trails through the park so it was really easy to see everything. Although my feet kinda hurt now…

We're at 7 x 8.

Fifty-six? I don't get it.

Nope, you got it fine. We're in the town of Fifty-six, Arkansas. We just saw **Blanchard Springs Caverns**.

What is that stuff?

It's called flowstone. There's even a river down there.

Where does it go?

It comes out the side of the mountain in a waterfall, into **Mirror Lake** below.

So cool.

Very. 58 degrees, to be exact.

Shouldn't it be 56?

Sister Cities Around the World

You can always count on your sisters, right? That's probably what the U.S. government was thinking in 1956, when it started the Sister Cities program. A lot of countries were still torn up from World War II. The program was a great way to rebuild some good will between nations. After all, what better way to get to know people than to be officially "related"?

Liverpool, England

Shoham, Israel

Kaolack, Senegal

Kanifing, The Gambia

Sister Cities of Memphis

Kanifing (right) is a town in The Gambia, a country in West Africa. It's just outside a large urban area called Serrekunda. The area is located on the coast of the Atlantic Ocean, and it's a cool place to visit. Another Memphis sister city, **Kaolack, Senegal** (below), is located about 60 miles to the northeast of Kanifing.

Technically, Memphis became "friends" (not sisters) with **Liverpool, England**, in 2004. But these two could be town twins. Both cities have had a huge influence on rock 'n' roll. Memphis has a long list of musical greats that lived or worked here. And Liverpool is home to The Beatles, one of the 20th century's greatest rock bands.

The latest addition to the family is **Shoham, Israel**. It became sisters with Memphis in 2017. Memphis has a strong Jewish community, so it made sense to team up with the Jewish city in the Middle East. Students in both countries write letters back and forth to get to know each other.

FIND OUT MORE!

Books, Websites, and More!

Books

Anastasio, Dina. *Where Is the Mississippi River?* Penguin Workshop, 2017.

Cunningham, Laura. *The Ghostly Tales of Memphis.* Arcadia Children's Books, 2021.

Duncan, Alice Faye. *Memphis, Martin, and the Mountaintop: The Sanitation Strike of 1968.* Calkins Creek, 2018.

Edgers, Geoff. *Who Was Elvis Presley?* Penguin Workshop, 2007.

Kelley, K.C. *Memphis Grizzlies.* Child's World, 2019.

McDaniel, Melissa. *Tennessee.* Children's Press, 2018.

Web Sites

City of Memphis
https://www.memphistn.gov

Memphis Travel
https://www. memphistravel.com

We Are Memphis
https://www. wearememphis.com

Graceland
https://www. graceland.com

Beale Street
https://www. bealestreet.com

National Civil Rights Museum
https://www. civilrightsmuseum.org

Photo Credits and Thanks

Photos from Dreamstime, Shutterstock, or Wikimedia unless otherwise noted. AP Photo: Charles Kelly 20 (2); Matt Peterson 41. Newscom: Karen Focht/Zumapress 30. Focus on Football: 64 top.

Artwork: LemonadePixel. Maps (6-7): Jessica Nevins.

Thanks to our pals Nancy Ellwood, Kait Leggett, and the fine folks at Arcadia!

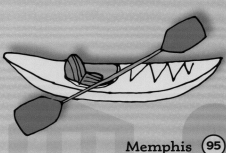

Thanks for Visiting

MEMPHIS

Come Back Soon!